"I tell you the truth, wherever the gospel is preached throughout the world, what she has done will also be told, in memory of her."

*Mark 14:9 NIV*

**MARY MAGDALENE**
*A woman who showed her gratitude*
Retold by Marlee Alex
Illustrated by José Pérez Montero
© Copyright 1987 by Scandinavia
Publishing House, Nørregade 32, DK-1165 Copenhagen K.
English-language edition published 1988
through special arrangement with Scandinavia
by Wm. B. Eerdmans Publishing Co.,
255 Jefferson Ave. S.E., Grand Rapids, Michigan 49503
All rights reserved
Printed in Hong Kong
ISBN 0-8028-5029-4

# Presenting the Outstanding Women of the Bible

The Bible is the story of God's dealings with his people. This story is like a picture God painted for all the world to see. God wanted to show everyone, everywhere, how much he loves ordinary people, and how he can make wonderful things happen through ordinary lives.

Israel was a nation with laws and traditions which gave men the leadership in government and family life. However, Israel's history is full of stories of women. Some of these women rose to become leaders. Others shaped and changed the life of their nation as they stayed in the background. These stories stress the unique influence women can have on history.

In Israel, the influence of women might have been limited by the customs and laws of their country, or by personal things such as the amount of money they had, the type of education, their husband's position, or the number of children in the family. But in these stories we meet woman after woman who, in spite of outward hindrances, was limited only by the degree of her faith in God or by the degree of her determination to use the gifts he gave her.

We hope this book will make you eager to be used by God, and help you to believe more than ever before that you can be all God made you to be.

# Mary Magdalene

## A woman who showed her gratitude

Retold by
Marlee Alex

Illustrated by
José Pérez
Montero

William B. Eerdmans Publishing Company
Grand Rapids, Michigan

The towers of Jerusalem, usually splashed in sunlight at that time of day, were wrapped in gray. A chill pervaded the city. Mary Magdalene shivered as she trudged up a hillside just outside the city wall. She pulled her cloak tightly around her shoulders but felt no warmer, for her heart was as cold as the wind. To Mary it seemed an eternity before she reached the hilltop of Golgotha, "The Place of the Skull." It was not a hill people climbed over in order to get to the other side. Golgotha was climbed for one of two reasons: to die or to watch someone else die.

"After this, nothing in the world can ever make things right again," murmured Mary to herself. Her words flew away through the turbulent air. No one heard what she said.

Several other women stood huddled together on the hilltop. When she reached them, Mary Magdalene felt brokenhearted and began to sob. A second woman, also named Mary, stood close by. But the gentle eyes of this woman revealed acceptance of what she witnessed, in spite of the terrible suffering. Two other women were clinging to each other for comfort. But Mary Magdalene could find no comfort.

The Roman soldiers milling about had no sympathy for the women. "These women should be forced to leave," one of them muttered.

Another soldier laughed in return, "No one should be allowed to mourn for this phony Jewish king."

The sky grew darker and raindrops spattered upon the sparse grass. Mary Magdalene looked up at the rough wooden cross standing between two other crosses on the top of Golgotha. The cross was the Roman method of putting criminals to death. Mary watched as the Person she loved more than anyone else in the world, a Man called Jesus, hung dying upon that center cross. He was in tremendous pain. His chest heaved as Mary watched. It seemed to her He was trying to catch His breath in order to speak.

7

Mary Magdalene moved closer to the foot of Jesus' cross. From the day she first met Jesus she had stayed as close as possible to Him. She had followed Him everywhere, helping His disciples in practical ways, listened carefully to His teaching, and witnessed miracle after miracle as He ministered to sick and sad people. Now, even as Jesus died, Mary wanted to be close to Him and hear any last words He might say. But instead, Mary's ears were filled with the sounds of hoarse laughter and crude jokes hurled at Jesus by the Roman soldiers, Jewish leaders, and even one of the thieves hanging on the cross beside Him.

Suddenly Jesus cried out, but not toward those waiting impatiently for Him to die. He cried toward heaven itself, "Father, forgive these people, for they do not understand what they are doing."

Mary Magdalene gasped. She thought to herself, "I cannot have heard Him right! Or did I? Did I really hear Him ask God to forgive these hypocrites, these murderers? No, Jesus! You brought only healing and mercy to the world! They are guilty." Mary wanted to cry out loud, "No! Never! Never forgive them for this!"

Before Mary could choke out the bitter words, however, her mind was flooded with memories. It was not so very long ago, since she herself had received God's forgiveness. At that time it had seemed to her as incredible as His words did now. Yet it had tasted sweet as honey when Jesus looked directly into her eyes and promised, "Your sins are forgiven!"

She had thought, "No man has ever dared look into my eyes at all. And certainly no one else has ever looked at me with acceptance, forgiveness or a love like this."

The only glances Mary Magdalene had ever drawn from men were lustful; from other women she had received only scorn. Children had usually looked at her in fear or curiosity, while their mothers had hurried them off in opposite directions or across the street. Mary never had a hope of raising a family of her own or having the kind of life most people take for granted.

For as long as she could remember she had been tormented by a demon and ruled by its wicked fancies. No one in her hometown of Magdala knew how it had started. But Mary had grown up, a homeless girl, known for her fits of rage and for the way she earned a living by selling her body to please men.

People had occasionally hissed at Mary in the street, "For God's sake, girl, take hold of yourself and start behaving decently!" Little had they realized how greatly she had wished she could do right instead of wrong. There were times when she had tried to master the demon within her and turn from her sinful way of life, the only kind of life she had ever known.

At one such time Mary had tried her hardest to drive the demon out of her soul and to clean up her life. For a while, her efforts had worked. But just when she had seemed closest to becoming a respectable person, the demon returned. Finding her life clean, yet empty, it had moved right back into its old home again. But this time it had brought six other demons with it. And these six were far worse than the first one.

13

Then Mary's life had become more miserable than ever. There were days she had struggled against the demons, but whenever the struggle grew too fierce, she had lost complete control of her body and mind. Thrown into a wild frenzy at those times, Mary Magdalene would writhe on the ground until all her strength had been drained. It had happened again and again until the last remnant of peace within her had finally been destroyed.

There had been one old woman in Magdala who had pitied Mary, but she had no idea how to help her. Nevertheless, Mary felt she knew at least one truth: no one would ever truly love her.

Then something totally unexpected had happened. Jesus of Nazareth had crossed her path in Magdala. As he passed within an arm's reach of her, the seven demons had begun to scream and wrestle with each other, shaking Mary's body as never before. The townspeople following Jesus had learned to keep out of Mary's way and ignore her. And not even Jesus had seemed to notice her that day. He had disappeared in the crowd.

Finally Mary had collapsed on the dusty street. By the time she had recovered, no one else was around. The crowds had dissipated into other streets and alleys. Jesus had already left town. But right away Mary had known something was different; her body and mind were at peace, no longer haunted by the evil spirits. They had been driven away by the very presence of Jesus.

Mary had picked herself up off the street in Magdala that day wondering, "What happened? Can I be sure the demons are gone for good? They will most likely return unless the emptiness in my soul is filled with something better." Mary had known that trying to live a decent life on her own or "be good" would not change things. So she had asked everyone she met, "Who was that Man? Where was He from? How can I find Him?"

They had answered, "He is called Jesus. He is a prophet from Nazareth who claims to be the Son of God." Mary knew holy men could have her stoned to death for the sinful way she lived. But that day she made a decision, "I would rather face death than the terror of the returning demons. I'm going to find that Man and talk to Him."

Many weeks passed before Mary had heard the news, "Jesus has returned."

"There is a rumor He will dine tonight at the home of a Jewish leader," an old woman had told her. "Ha! That's a switch! He usually eats with tax collectors and sinners!" The woman had laughed spitefully. She had not even recognized Mary as the young woman who so recently had been known as the worst sinner in town.

Mary had continued questioning people until she found the house where Jesus would be dining. A crowd had begun to gather around the door and windows. Mary had pressed through the crowd and into the doorway. "I would rather die at the feet of this Man than be tormented for the rest of my life," she had whispered.

Without thinking she had pushed her way right into the room where Jesus was reclining on a couch by the dinner table. Once in His presence, a surge of hope and gratitude had welled up within her.

Mary had sunk to her knees at the end of the couch as tears had spilled from her eyes onto Jesus' bare feet. The tears had glistened like diamonds. Surprisingly, Jesus had not made any attempt to move away from her. Mary had dried away the tears from Jesus' feet with her long dark hair, then began to gently kiss his feet and ankles. Clasping the small, white marble bottle that had always hung on a belt around her waist, Mary had poured its last drops of perfume onto His feet and rubbed them into His skin.

While Jesus had not even been embarrassed by what Mary had done, His Jewish host had felt differently. He had grown paler by the minute, for gradually it had dawned on him that this was the woman well known in Magdala for the wicked life she led. He was horrified. "If Jesus were really sent from God," he had thought to himself, "He would know this woman is a sinner. He would never have allowed her to touch Him like this."

Jesus had interrupted the man's thoughts. "A certain man owed a friend 500 coins," He said. "Another man owed the same friend 50 coins. Neither of the men was able to pay back the money he owed. So their friend told them, 'All right, neither of you have to pay me back. You are forgiven your debts.'"

Jesus had turned to the Jewish leader. "Now which of these two men do you suppose will love his friend the most?" He asked.

The Jewish leader had answered, "Well, the one who owed the most money because he would have the most for which to be thankful."

Jesus had looked directly into the eyes of His host. "You are correct," He whispered. "And did you see what this woman has just done? When I came into your house you did not offer Me the favor of a basin of water and a towel with which to clean My dusty feet. But she has washed them with her tears and dried them with her hair. You did not greet Me with a kiss on My cheek, but she has kissed My feet and used up her last drops of ointment upon them.

"This woman is driven to express her love because she has much for which to be thankful. But as for the person who thinks he can get along fine by himself or doesn't need God's forgiveness, his love for Me will be weak and feeble. And he will be unwilling to show even the least bit of gratitude."

The face of the Jewish leader had flushed pink. But Jesus had turned around to Mary and said, "Woman, your sins are forgiven. The faith you have displayed in Me today has saved you. Go in peace."

As Mary left the house of the Jewish leader that day she had heard the crowd behind her murmuring and questioning each other, "Who is this Man, Jesus, who thinks He has the right to forgive sins?"

Mary Magdalene stood at the foot of the cross on Golgotha where these memories swept through her mind. The wind picked up strength. The day became darker still. Mary's thoughts were jarred to the present. Jesus suddenly cried out above her, "Father, into Your hands I commit My Spirit." Then His body lurched forward, the nails tore the flesh in His hands, and He fell limp upon the cross.

Mary was startled. It didn't seem possible Jesus could be dead. For the first time she drew closer to the other women on the hilltop. As Jesus' body was at last removed from the cross they followed Joseph, the man who carried it, to a new tomb not far away. The women watched as Joseph wrapped Jesus' body in linen and laid it in the clean stone tomb.

"So this is how it is to end," whispered one of the women.

Mary interrupted, "Only days ago we followed Jesus from Galilee and listened to the happy shouts of children here in Jerusalem. 'Hosanna! Hosanna to the king, the son of David!' they were shouting."

"Now the parents of these same children have executed our King, Jesus, like a common thief," continued a third woman.

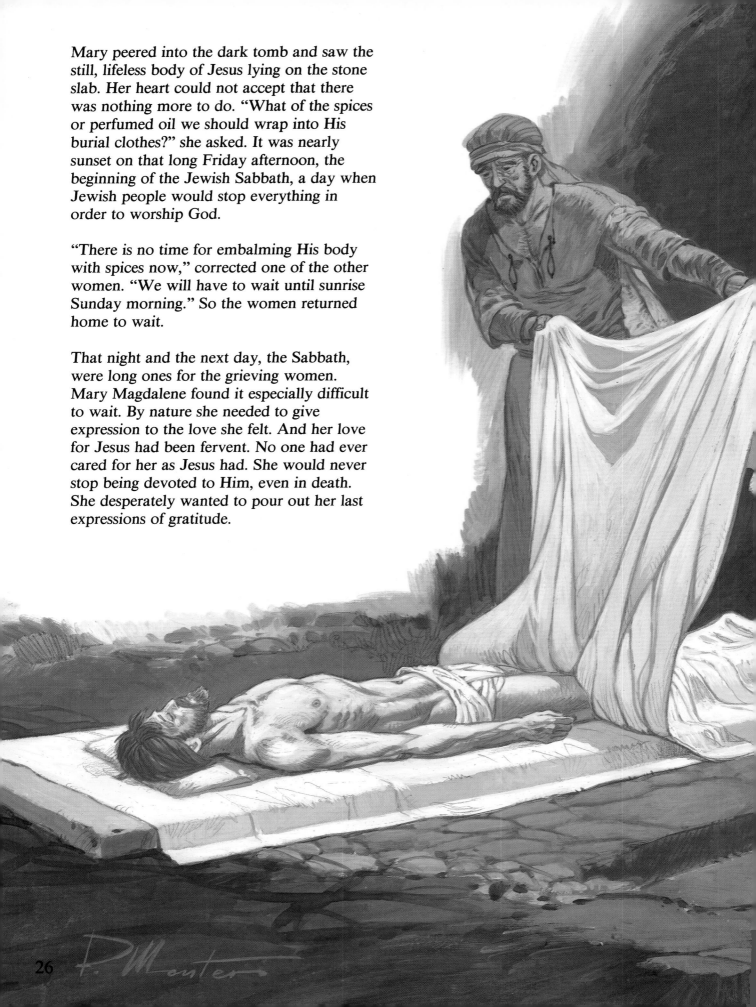

Mary peered into the dark tomb and saw the still, lifeless body of Jesus lying on the stone slab. Her heart could not accept that there was nothing more to do. "What of the spices or perfumed oil we should wrap into His burial clothes?" she asked. It was nearly sunset on that long Friday afternoon, the beginning of the Jewish Sabbath, a day when Jewish people would stop everything in order to worship God.

"There is no time for embalming His body with spices now," corrected one of the other women. "We will have to wait until sunrise Sunday morning." So the women returned home to wait.

That night and the next day, the Sabbath, were long ones for the grieving women. Mary Magdalene found it especially difficult to wait. By nature she needed to give expression to the love she felt. And her love for Jesus had been fervent. No one had ever cared for her as Jesus had. She would never stop being devoted to Him, even in death. She desperately wanted to pour out her last expressions of gratitude.

Early Sunday morning before the other women awoke, Mary got up in the darkness and gathered the carefully prepared spices and oils she had made ready before sundown on Friday. In the glow of the approaching dawn she made her way to the tomb on the hillside where Jesus' body lay. Along the way she wondered, "Who will roll away the stone? How will I be able to enter?"

But arriving at the tomb, Mary was amazed to find the large rock had already been rolled away. An angel was sitting on top of it, although Mary did not recognize him as a messenger from God. The angel said to Mary, "Why are you looking in a grave for a man who is alive?"

Startled and confused, Mary bent down and took a long look into the place where she had watched Joseph lay the body of Jesus. The tomb was empty. "Someone has taken His body away," she exclaimed.

"See, Jesus is not here!" the angel announced. "He is alive!"

Mary could neither understand nor believe what she was hearing. She turned and went back the way she had come, trying to make sense of the events of the past three days. Then she noticed a Man approaching her on the path. The sun was rising over the lowest trees behind Him. The radiant sunbeams shone into her eyes as she called out, "You must be the gardener here. Sir, if you have taken the body of Jesus, please tell me where it is. I have come to anoint it with oil and place these spices in His grave clothes."

The man on the narrow path stepped directly in front of the shining sun. His face was full of light, His expression pure like the sun itself. "Mary!" He said. That voice chimed like music in Mary's ears. It was a voice she recognized, for no one had ever said her name in quite that way except for ... Jesus!

"Lord!" Mary exclaimed. She ran to Him and fell at His feet.

"Wait, Mary," Jesus interrupted. "Don't touch Me yet. I haven't yet ascended to My Father in heaven. But go and tell My other friends you have met Me. Tell those who followed Me to wait in Jerusalem. I'll meet them there soon." Then Jesus disappeared from Mary's sight. Her feet nearly flew as she hurried back to the disciples to tell what she had seen.

A s a follower of Jesus Christ, Mary Magdalene witnessed that the only people Jesus had no power to forgive were those who believed they were already good enough or those who were too proud to recognize Him as God's Son. When Mary expressed her faith in Jesus and received God's forgiveness she was filled with a fervent love for Him.

Mary continuously fed her love for Jesus with acts of gratitude and devotion. She became the first person to meet Jesus after He rose from the dead. She brought the message of joy to Jesus' friends and set an example for all who wish to bring joy to the heart of Jesus Himself.

# Read the story of Mary in your Bible:

Then Mary took about a pint of pure nard, an expensive perfume; she poured it on Jesus' feet and wiped his feet with her hair. And the house was filled with the fragrance of the perfume.

*John 12:3 NIV*

Some of those present were saying indignantly to one another, "Why this waste of perfume? It could have been sold for more than a year's wages and the money given to the poor." And they rebuked her harshly. "Leave her alone," said Jesus. "Why are you bothering her? She has done a beautiful thing to me. The poor you will always have with you, and you can help them any time you want. But you will not always have me. She did what she could. She poured perfume on my body beforehand to prepare for my burial. **I tell you the truth, wherever the gospel is preached throughout the world, what she has done will also be told, in memory of her.**"

*Mark 14:4-11 NIV*

"Therefore, I tell you, her many sins have been forgiven — for she loved much. But he who has been forgiven little loves little." Then Jesus said to her, "Your sins are forgiven."

*Luke 7:47-48 NIV*

When Jesus rose early on the first day of the week, he appeared first to Mary Magdalene.

*Mark 16:9a*

See also:
Matthew 27:55-56, Mark 16:1-9, John 19:25, John 20:1-18